Reinaldo Domingos

Money Boy
Family dreams

1st Edition

About the series

The series "Money Boy" is a children's adaptation based upon the DSOP Financial Education Methodology, conceived by master, professor, educator, and financial therapist Reinaldo Domingos.

The series is part of the DSOP Financial Education Program that ranges from grammar school to college. It consists of 30 didactic volumes (15 textbooks and 15 teacher's books) and six paradidactic volumes that comprise subjects of family, diversity, sustainability, autonomy, and citizenship.

In addition to the books, the schools that adopt the DSOP Financial Education Program are entitled to pedagogical training, financial education workshops for teachers, lectures for the students and the community, and access to the school website (portalescolas.dsop.com.br), which consists of class plans, interactive activities (games), videos, and exclusive access to students, teachers, parents, and school managers.

For further information, please visit www.dsop.com.br/escolas or contact a local franchisee in your area by searching on our website www.dsop.com.br/franquia.

What's happening

This is this sweet story's main character. Intertwined in a light, involving narrative, there are powerful lessons about the human relationship with money and with our own dreams.

Born to a humble family, this boy soon learns to value the coins he earns, saving them in a piggybank in order to achieve the things he wants some day.

Meanwhile, he hears words of wisdom from his mother, about making choices, being patient and keeping the faith, as he grasps the notion of keeping a small part of what he has to make his dreams come true in the future. At the same time the world unveils before his bright eyes, he keeps learning other important things: not all of our dreams can be purchased with money.

Regardless of age, readers of Money Boy will have the opportunity to revisit the children they once were, tracking down the way of this apprenticeship page after page. By transforming habits, taking new attitudes and reeducating themselves financially, in the end of the book they will reinvigorate their hope and their ability to dream.

©Editora DSOP, 2016
©Reinaldo Domingos, 2015

Author
Reinaldo Domingos

Illustration and graphic design
Ariel Fajtlowicz

Text editor
Renata de Sá
Samir Thomaz

Art editor
Joyce Thomaz

Editorial production
Amanda Torres

English language version
Joan Rumph
Milena Cavichiolo

All rights reserved to Editora DSOP
Av. Paulista, 726 - Cj. 1210 - Bela Vista
ZIP Code: 01310-910 - Brazil - São Paulo - SP
Phone: 55 11 3177-7800
www.editoradsop.com.br

Dados Internacionais de Catalogação na Publicação (CIP)
(Câmara Brasileira do Livro, SP, Brasil)

```
Domingos, Reinaldo
    Money boy : family dreams / Reinaldo Domingos ;
illustration Ariel Fajtlowicz ; translation Joan
Rumph e Milena Cavichiolo. -- São Paulo : Editora
DSOP, 2015.

    Título original: O menino do dinheiro : sonhos
de família
    ISBN 978-85-8276-116-8

    1. Dinheiro - Literatura infantojuvenil
2. Finanças - Literatura infantojuvenil
I. Fajtlowicz, Ariel. II. Título.


14-11829                                    CDD-028.5
```

Índices para catálogo sistemático:

1. Educação financeira : Literatura infantil
   028.5
2. Educação financeira : Literatura infantojuvenil
   028.5

Contents

A kid who knows what he wants 7

The red piggy 11

A very special birthday 15

Every other day 21

Waiting and being patient 25

The perfect idea 29

A lesson from son to father 35

Questions without answers 41

A son's advice 45

Nothing like a day after another 49

The long-awaited jingling 53

A kid who knows what he wants

In a peaceful, faraway town called Lagoa Branca, lived a small boy named Ray. When he was born, he was quite thin and frail. He used to cry a lot in his first months of life, more than babies usually do, as if he had something to tell the world right from the start.

Once, after his mother tried everything to calm him down, his grandmother said, "I think this boy is hungry. Why don't you feed him some extra milk so he'll stop crying?"

The mother gave her son another bottle of milk, which the boy drank up and fell asleep for almost 24 hours! When the mother saw the baby breathing quietly and the peaceful expression on his face as he slept, her worries vanished.

"Thank goodness. I think all he wanted was more milk after all. Gee, this boy is really quite something. So young and yet he's already found a way to get what he wants," said the proud mother.

Ray's early years went by without many difficulties. He grew up playing in the backyard dirt, collecting stones and leaves of all possible shapes and colors. He watched the insects walking across the ground in their daily labor and admired the clouds creating figures in the sky, always under his mother's close sight.

Ray's father left for work early in the morning, so the boy saw very little of him during the daytime. The father's name was Mr. Unaware and he worked as a railway engineer, operating train cars up and down the railroad tracks loaded with all sorts of goods. The train cars left the town fully loaded and came back empty, or sometimes the other way around. This happened every day, always following the same timetable.

Ray enjoyed hearing the sounds the train made as it approached the station at the end of the day. This signal meant his father would be home soon. However, when Mr. Unaware arrived home, he always looked tired and had no desire to play with his son. The father complained about his hard life, but the boy did not quite realize what it meant. After all, Ray spent his days sleeping, eating, playing, and dreaming. The boy loved to dream! As far back as he could remember his head was full of stories, questions, and dreams.

Despite not spending much time with his father and not having siblings, Ray did not feel lonely. His mother kept him company. She looked after him and never left him alone.

Even when she visited her customers, door to door, in order to sell her handmade jewelry and perfumes, Mrs. Foresight brought her son along. The boy delighted in all those wonderful bright colors his mother put on display for her customers. He stood to the side, and listened to the rustling sounds produced by the small bags of jewelry. The neighbors squealed with excitement as she approached them with goods to sell, not to mention the exquisite scent of perfumes.

One day, on their way back from visiting customers Ray asked his mother to buy him some candy and ice cream.

"As long as you remain a good boy, I will buy you either candy or ice cream," she said. "You may choose only one. You must learn to make choices, son. In this life, you cannot always have everything you want."

The boy listened to her carefully, but did not understand why he could not have candy and ice cream on the same day. They were both goodies. Frequently on their way back home, Mrs. Foresight would spare some coins of different shapes and sizes and put them in the palm of his hand. The clerks at the candy store and at the ice cream truck already knew it. As Ray approached them, they would promptly ask him, "So kid, what's it going to be today, ice cream or candy?"

During the nice warm evenings, with the gentle wind blowing amongst the trees, a look of confusion appeared on the boy's face, because he really wanted to have both things at the same time. Only during the cold days of winter, when the dewdrops turned into small ice crystals on the grass, could he easily make up his mind. He chose the candy, because his mother would not allow him to have ice cream.

No matter which choice Ray made he always returned home very happy, for those coins were precious. He could trade them in for delicious things such as ice cream and candy.

The red piggy

On his fifth birthday, Ray started to ask his mother the same thing he always asked her.

"Mom, since it's my birthday, it's time for some ice cream and candy. We'd agreed to–," but Mrs. Foresight interrupted him.

"Today is a very special day and I'll give you something far more important than ice cream and candy," she said.

She reached into her purse, pulled out a small round package and handed it to her son. Ray immediately tore open the wrapping paper and became confused, staring down at a red piggy with a slit in its back.

"What is this, mom? A cracked piggy?" he said while turning the piggy upside down.

"This is a piggy bank, son. It's your birthday present," she replied. "Now that you are five years old, you have to learn a very important lesson—one that will remain with you for your entire life. The boy looked up waiting to hear more about his unusual gift, but his mother began walking away quietly.

Finally, she turned and said, "You will learn the entire lesson when we return home after visiting customers, okay?"

Ray nodded and followed her, grabbing the piggy in his hand and wondering how important a pig could ever become.

On the way home, as soon as he saw the ice cream truck and the candy shop, the boy begged his mother, "Today, you will buy me ice cream and candy, right? Please, it is my birthday! Buy them!"

Mrs. Foresight stopped as she reached for the coins in her little purse.

"Son, today we are beginning a new phase in your life, and it will be very important for your future. Here are your coins," she said. "There is enough for one ice cream and some candy, but I want you to make a choice. You are going to buy either the ice cream or the candy."

A look of disappointment fell over Ray's face. He did not understand why she would deprive him of things he enjoyed. After all, it is his birthday. But his mother insisted, so the boy chose the ice cream this time. The few coins his mother gave him only paid for the ice cream. He glanced at the candy store with sadness in his eyes.

Walking back to his mother and still eating his ice cream, his mother surprised him by handing him the rest of the coins. Ray even thought she had changed her mind, but before he could say anything, she made it clear.

"These coins are for you to fulfill other wishes in your life. In the future, keep them in your piggy bank and leave them there until you have collected lots of them."

Ray quickly grabbed the coins and put them in his pocket, afraid his ice cream would melt. After he finished eating, he slid the coins one by one into the piggy bank. The coins made a nice jingle as they dropped into the piggy bank. It made

Ray feel a little better. He looked at his mother and thanked her even though he could not quite understand the purpose of collecting coins.

Mrs. Foresight, a very conscientious and protective mother, used to tell him, "Trust me. Everything I tell you is for your own good."

Ray got excited every time he added coins to the piggy. Something told him that the jingling noise was the beginning of many good things to come.

A very special birthday

From that day on, Ray began saving coins in his piggy bank. It grew heavier day by day. As time went by, he noticed that his mother had a habit of saving money—not coins, but one or more dollar bills. Her bank was a huge jar she kept on top of the kitchen cabinet.

Throughout the year, the boy did exactly what his mother had told him to do. Each afternoon after they finished visiting customers, his mother gave him coins, which he added to his piggy bank. Soon, the sound of jingling coins began to fade. At the same time, the piggy became heavier and heavier, and harder to hold.

Occasionally, Ray would ask, "Mom, when there's no room for more coins in the piggy, what should I do?"

Her answer was always the same. "Let's wait until then and we'll figure out what to do!"

A year went by and, as expected, the piggy bank became so full it was impossible to slip another coin into it. On Ray's sixth birthday, the mother asked him to bring her the piggy and they both sat at the kitchen table to have a new chat.

She began by saying, "Son, I want to congratulate you for doing what we had agreed to do. You kept saving the coins I gave you."

The boy was happy to have made his mother proud and he continued to listen to what she had to say.

"Just like you've been telling me, your piggy is full. Now it's time for you to know how much you've saved," she explained.

Then the mother took a hammer and smashed open the piggy, breaking it into a thousand tiny pieces. Ray was amazed at the massive amount of coins inside the piggy that now were scattered all over the table and onto the floor.

"Wow, mom! So many coins! I didn't realize I'd saved that much!" shouted Ray.

At the time, the boy did not know how to count. Mrs. Foresight made up a fun way to separate the coins and divided them according to sizes and colors. Ray loved it. He could tell them apart by placing them into small piles with ten coins of each kind.

Eventually, small piles of coins of several different sizes and colors lay spread across the table. Mrs. Foresight organized the collection and said, "Son, there are nineteen piles of coins. Now, think of a wish you want to come true using the coins."

Ray pictured himself with pockets full of candy and holding an ice cream cone in each hand.

"Mom, I'd like to have two ice cream cones and a bag full of candy," he said unaware of what her reaction would be.

"That's alright," she replied, placing two piles of coins close to him.

"And what else?" she asked, staring at him firmly.

Ray's eyes gleamed at that unexpected question.

"So, can I have something else?" he asked.

"Sure can. What about a toy?" she suggested.

"Can I have a soccer ball?" he asked.

"Of course," she said, separating another pile of coins and placing it close to the boy.

Ray got so excited when he noticed there were several other piles of coins remaining on the table that he decided to take a chance and ask for something more.

"Mom, can I get a toy car, too?" he asked.

Mrs. Foresight looked at him and spoke in a lovely tone of voice:
"Son, remember what I told you before you began saving the coins?"

Ray nodded, a little ashamed, because he knew what that tone of voice meant.

"You've got to learn to make choices, son. In this life, you cannot always have all that you want." He was about to say he was sorry when his mother added, "Besides learning to make choices, son, you've got to be patient and wait for some things to be accomplished. When you grow a little older, you'll understand what I'm telling you now."

There was no time for sadness. She stood up, reached for the jar where she kept her money and took a small package from inside it, and handed it over to her son.

Ray tore the wrapping paper off the package and flashed a great big smile. The gift was a blue piggy bank, even larger than the previous one.

"Now that you've made your choices, take the rest of the coins and put them inside this new piggy," said his mother. "That way it will fill up quicker and you'll be able to achieve other wishes."

The boy was super happy and he quickly slid the coins inside the blue piggy. The jingling came back, just like the smile on his face.

Mrs. Foresight cleaned up the mess from the broken piggy bank and told her son to keep the new piggy bank in his room. They were going to go out to buy candy, ice cream, and a soccer ball.

Ray could hardly sleep that night. That birthday sure was a special one. He went to sleep thinking about all the dreams he could achieve if only he could keep saving his coins.

Every other day

Time went by and Ray became more excited every day, making a game out of saving coins. He even stopped thinking about ice cream and candy and began imagining the things he could achieve when his piggy bank was full.

One day, after his mother had given him some coins as usual, he did not stop to shop for goodies on the way back home. The clerk at the candy store found that strange and asked his mother if the kid was doing fine.

"Yes, as far as I know," she answered, glancing oddly at her son. Later on, she asked the boy, "Son, why didn't you want to buy candy today?"

"I've decided to stop spending my coins every single day. Instead, I'm going to buy goodies every other day. That way my piggy bank will fill up faster," Ray said.

Mrs. Foresight could not believe it. Her son surprised her with such a mature attitude for his age.

"Well done, son. Eating candy every day is not a healthy habit either. The less you eat of it, the better it is for you," she said, giving him a hug. "I see that you're learning the importance of saving a small amount of what you earn to achieve future dreams. If you keep that pace, soon you will be the one teaching me things!"

Ray was so happy he could barely stand still. After all, he considered Mrs. Foresight the world's smartest woman. He walked as though he was floating above the ground, lifted by a balloon. That feeling made him think of something that had never occurred to him before. He realized that the habit of saving coins was bringing him good things and good things only. He was happy, his mother was happy, and he had a good feeling when he realized his coins were there at his fingertips.

With the money he saved, Ray would be able to make his dreams come true. It was simply a matter of time. Waiting, just like his mother would wait for the right time to pick the vegetables she grew in their backyard. Only the boy's father kept sad and silent, repeating that life was harder each day that passed. Ray wished his father was as optimistic and reliant as Mrs. Foresight. Then he came up with a wonderful idea.

Money Boy - Family dreams

Waiting and being patient

Ray continued to save his coins. Soon the blue piggy bank became completely full with no room left for another coin. His birthday was still some months ahead.

One day, he took the initiative and told his mother, "Mom, I think it's time we opened the piggy because there's no room for savings anymore."

Mrs. Foresight, being a very clever woman, said she had a better idea. Ray just had to wait for the next day. The boy begged his mother to tell him about her idea, but she wouldn't say a word.

"Son, I've told you before and I'm repeating it now. You have to learn to be patient. Everything in its time."

Waiting and being patient seemed to be Mrs. Foresight's favorite words. Ray was used to hearing her repeating them. He knew it was difficult to make his mother rush into things. However, he had no other choice than to be patient and wait for the next day to come.

Early the next day, Mrs. Foresight reached into the drawer and removed yet another piggy bank—this time, a white one, a little larger than the blue piggy.

"There is still some time before your next birthday," she told her son. "Meanwhile, you can be filling up this new piggy."

Ray didn't like his mother's idea that much. He really wanted to break open the piggy that was already full.

"But mom, how long will I be filling up piggies?" the boy complained. "You gave me a red one, a blue one, and now a white piggy. Soon there will be no colors left!

Mrs. Foresight frowned with a look of disappointment after hearing her son. In a certain way, she knew the boy was right. However, at that moment, she could not come up with a better answer to give him.

"Do as I say and I promise you on your birthday we will begin a new stage in your life," she said.

"But I will not be able to do things the way I want them to happen," Ray replied.

Intrigued, the mother asked, "What is it that you want to happen your way?"

Ray felt so ashamed that he did not want to tell his mother about his idea.

"Nothing, it's nothing. Besides, we're even now. You've got to wait until my birthday before I can tell you," he said with a grin.

"Okay then, that's a deal," said Mrs. Foresight, trying to hide her curiosity.

The perfect idea

The long-awaited day came. On a sunny Friday, Ray became seven years old. He no longer looked thin and frail, but had become a strong kid with a bright smile and lively eyes.

Mrs. Foresight gazed at him with happiness and wonder. It made her proud to see her son growing up in his gentle, reassuring way, day after day. For a long time, Mrs. Foresight had prayed that her son would have a bright future, and she felt her prayers had been answered.

As soon as Ray finished his breakfast, he spoke up. "That's it, mom. Now that I've eaten, let's open my piggy," he said anxiously.

Mrs. Foresight barely could answer, because the boy had already made his way to the room and came back carrying a piggy in each hand.

"All right then, but let's open only the blue piggy, which is full. The other one will keep on getting coins as usual," she said, holding a hammer in her hand.

Ray nodded his head in agreement and soon his second piggy shattered into pieces before him. Together, he and his mother piled up the coins, just as they had done before. After counting all the coins, the mother asked the question the boy had spent the whole year waiting to answer.

"Son, what is the wish you want to come true this time?" she asked, expecting him to say ice cream and candy.

But she was very surprised when she heard his answer.

"I want to buy a new piggy bank, the largest one that we can find," he said assertively.

"I thought you did not want to hear about piggies anymore. Besides, your white piggy isn't even full," she said, feeling a bit confused.

"It's not for me, mom," Ray said.

"Who is it for then?" asked Mrs. Foresight with her hands on her hips.

"It's for daddy," answered the boy. "Perhaps this way he'll be able to make his wishes come true. Maybe he'll become happier, just like me," Ray explained.

Mrs. Foresight's eyes began to tear up. What a wonderful thing the boy had said, she thought to herself. She put her arms around her son and gave him a big, long hug.

Finally Mrs. Foresight spoke, "Well done, dear. Let's buy your father a piggy bank, too."

"You also have to choose something as a gift for yourself. It can be anything you like. You really deserve a nice present," she added, beaming with pride.

"Maybe a toy car, mom," said the boy. "But I don't want to use up all my coins, because I want to give daddy some, so he'll have coins to fill his piggy."

This time, Mrs. Foresight could barely contain her happiness. When did the little kid grow up to be such a mature boy that she didn't even notice it?

That thought reminded her of surprising news she had avoided telling him.

Drying her eyes and clearing her throat she said, "Well done, son. I believe your attitude has showed me it's about time you began a new stage in your life. You'll be starting school in a few months.

"School?" asked Ray a bit frightened.

"Son, it's about time. Besides, I believe I've taught you everything I can. You're a smart boy, who still has to learn a few more things that I'm not able to teach by myself.

"Sure you are, mom! Everything I know you taught me. I don't need any school!" said the boy, hiding under the kitchen table.

Mrs. Foresight bent down beneath the table to look at Ray.

"You know, son," she started to say. "Let me tell you something."

"Children are raised in the world, and the world is always much larger than our backyard. Being afraid is normal," she assured him. "We are always afraid of change, but change is necessary. Without changing and facing new things, one cannot grow up."

"Of course we do, mom," Ray insisted. "You keep saying I'm growing bigger every day."

"It's not a matter of size. I'm talking about inner growth, in the heart and in the mind, and school is very important. At school, you're going to meet new people, make new friends, and learn new games. All of this is very important for a healthy childhood," she stated.

"You cannot spend your whole childhood with me alone. It's about time you had new friends. In addition, being an eager learner such as you, I'm quite sure you will soon love the idea of going to school. Trust me on this one, too."

The boy stared at his mother and suddenly felt confident. For a reason he was not aware of, it seemed as though his mother was always right. He gave his mother a big, long hug, feeling the softness of her skin and the scent of her perfume.

As he stepped back, he became that same boy as before. Eventually he said, "Okay then, let's buy daddy's piggy now. I want to give it to him as soon as he comes home.

A lesson from son to father

Ray's heart began to pump faster when he heard the train whistle. He knew his father would soon be home, and he could hardly wait to give him his present. He was about to run to the front door when his mother stopped him.

"Son, take it easy. Wait for your father to arrive properly, take a shower, and relax. As soon as he has calmed down, you may give him your present. Do as I tell you and you won't regret it," she instructed.

Disappointed, Ray returned to his room and sat down on the floor with the piggy at his side, waiting for his father to come see him. Waiting there was even harder than waiting for his birthday to come. The boy began to daydream about what his father would do when he finished collecting all his coins in the piggy bank. Maybe he would buy a new leather wallet or a cell phone, or even tickets to a soccer game!

It was difficult for the boy to figure out his father's wishes. Mr. Unaware barely spoke. He kept saying life is hard or too expensive and that was all. Sure enough, life is expensive.

Ray did not even know if it was possible to exchange coins for a wallet, a cell phone or soccer tickets. Perhaps he needed dollar bills, like those his mother's customers exchanged for rings, earrings and perfumes. All of that remained a mystery for him. When he asked too many questions, his mother simply said, "Everything has its own time."

He thought about what she said earlier and, yes, it was time he started attending school. Maybe someone there would help him answer those questions that were spinning around in his head like birds flying over their nests.

Ray, deep in thought, didn't realize how much time had passed. Suddenly, he heard his mother calling out to him.

The boy stood still in the living room, staring at his father, waiting for him to wish him a happy birthday. Mr. Unaware didn't say a word.

"Daddy, aren't you forgetting something?" he asked.

Mr. Unaware didn't appear to realize what was going on, but soon he gave Ray a weak smile and said, "I haven't forgotten your birthday, son. It's just that I get even sadder on this day, because I can't buy you a nice present. Life is more expensive each day, and the money I make is not enough. Without the help of your mother, and the things that she sells, I don't know how our life would be.

Ray saw the sadness on his father's face and wanted to make him feel better. He gave his father the small package he was hiding behind his back.

Mr. Unaware surprised by the son's attitude asked, "What's this? It's your birthday and I'm getting the present?"

"Yeah, daddy," Ray answered with glimmering eyes. "I think this present will help cheer you up. Open it!"

Mr. Unaware appeared intrigued as he removed the paper. He looked up at Mrs. Foresight, who remained quiet.

"What am I going to do with this piggy, son?" asked the father.

"It's like this, daddy. Whenever you have an extra coin in your pocket, place it inside the piggy. Over time, it will be full of coins. Then you break it, count the coins you saved, and make a wish you want to come true with them."

Confused, yet moved, Mr. Unaware looked down at Ray.

"It's a good idea, son, but there's nothing left of my salary to save in the piggy," he said, handing it back to the boy.

"Salary? What's a salary, dad?" Ray asked.

Mr. Unaware began to grow impatient but he saw his son's eyes begging for an answer.

"Salary is the money people pay us at the end of the month for the work we do each day. I get up early and go to work precisely to earn the money that pays for our living expenses. That same money is what we use to buy our food, pay our bills, and all the things we need."

The boy smiled with excitement, even though he didn't fully understand the meaning of a salary. For the very first time, his father taught him something.

"Let's do this," Ray said eagerly. "Each time mom and I have some coins we will share them with you. I'll put a coin in my piggy and one in yours. Whenever you have some extra coins, you'll be able to save, too. If you don't, that's all right. For starters, take these coins."

Ray handed the father a bunch of coins from his pocket.

Mr. Unaware explained, "Son, it's a kind gesture, but I can't accept what little money you and your mother have sacrificed to give to me.

"But daddy, you've got to fill up your piggy," the boy insisted.

Mr Unaware appreciated his son's gift, still he didn't seem to understand the purpose behind it. "Well, I'll think it over, but I don't want your coins. I'll put the piggy on my bedside table and I'll put some coins in it if I can. Let's see if it works."

"Okay, daddy. I'll keep an eye on your piggy until it gets really full," Ray said.

"And what am I going to do with the coins when the piggy becomes full?" the father asked as he put the piggy on the coffee table.

"Like I said, you can make a dream come true. Just like mom has taught me," replied the boy.

 "I don't have a dream," the father started to say, when Mrs. Foresight called them for dinner.

Ray wanted to ask his father why he didn't have a dream, but he was afraid the question would make him upset. Instead, he ate dinner in silence with a new puzzle in his head to solve.

Money Boy - Family dreams

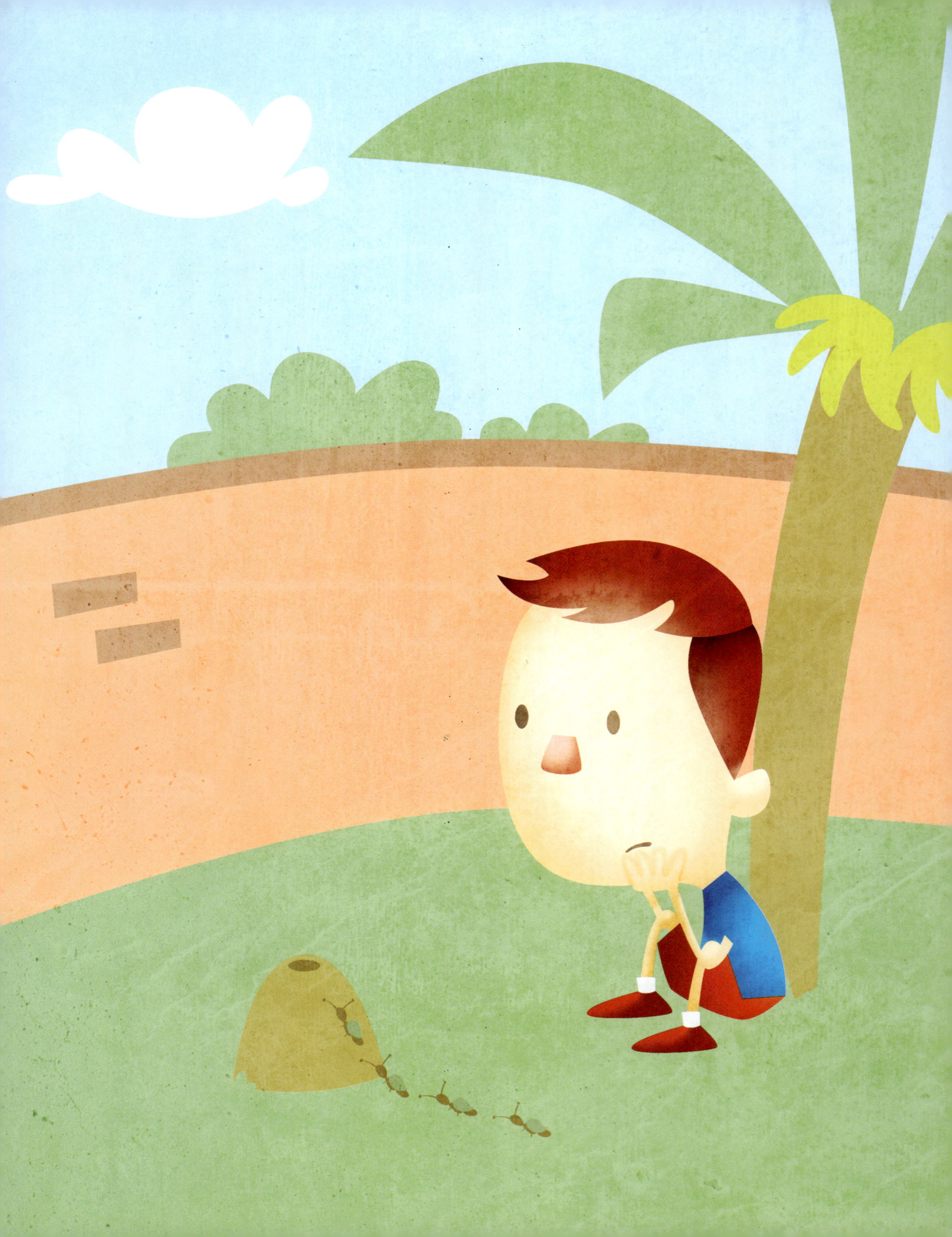

Questions without answers

The next day, the boy woke up and ran to his father's room. Mr. Unaware had already gone to work, but his piggy bank was still there. The boy held the piggy and tossed it in the air, anxious to hear the sound of coins jingling, promising good things. The piggy was silent.

Saddened because he thought his idea had failed, the boy did what he used to do whenever he was worried or had gotten angry. He had a talk with his mother, who was in the backyard watering the plants.

"Mom, yesterday I gave daddy a piggy bank, but he said he didn't have any coins to put in it. He also said life is hard and there's nothing left of his salary. Why does daddy keep saying life is hard?"

"Son, the life of an adult is sometimes a little complicated, because we have many responsibilities, especially when we have kids to take care of," said Mrs. Foresight while pulling weeds that grew among the kale plants.

The boy felt a lump in his throat, feeling that maybe it was his fault that his father was so sad.

"You mean daddy is sad and finds life hard just because he has a kid?" Ray asked nervously. Mrs. Foresight noticed the change in his voice at once. She immediately stopped what she was doing to focus on the conversation.

"Not exactly," she replied, rubbing her hands to remove the dirt. "What I'm saying is that people like your dad sometimes get sad and lose hope, because they forget how to dream. They're always worried with life's daily needs and forget how to create their own dreams."

"That's exactly what daddy said yesterday, mom! I told him he could make his dreams come true using his coins. Then he told me he didn't have any dreams. I just wonder how anyone could possibly live without dreams," said the boy.

"That's true, honey. Sometimes people leave their dreams behind and, all of a sudden, they realize they've lost the ability to dream. But, there's always time to change," said the mother.

The boy got a little confused, as he couldn't quite grasp what his mother was talking about. Mrs. Foresight noticed the concerned look on her son's face and tried to explain it further.

"For example, your father says he doesn't have any coins to put into the piggy, but he spends part of his salary on foolish things. If only he changed certain habits he could fill up the piggy faster than you," she said, turning back to her garden.

"Mom, that is the world's greatest idea. Why don't we tell him?" he asked.

"I've already tried to convince him several times, and it seems I haven't been able to. It's his attitude that has to change."

"What do you mean by attitude, mom?"

"Remember the day you decided not to eat candy every day and kept your coins instead?

"Yeah!" Ray admitted.

"That's it. That's an attitude you've taken," she said.

The boy stood still paying careful attention to what his mother was saying.

"That kind of attitude has helped me to make my dreams come true," she continued. "You see, son, it's up to your father to change. You should go play and stop worrying about stuff like that. The only things you need to be worried about, at least for a while, are your toys and games. Over the next year, you are going to focus on school," said Mrs. Foresight, putting an end to the conversation.

The boy sat beneath a huge tree, in the corner of the backyard, remembering the recent conversation with his mother.

While he watched little ants carrying, with difficulty, small leaves inside their anthill, he thought about his father telling him that life is hard. In a way, the sight of ants carrying leaves on their backs reminded him of his father pulling train cars up and down the tracks. Although, the ants didn't seem sad, he observed. On the contrary, they appeared to be content. He wondered if maybe the ants also find life harsh, carrying leaves larger than themselves, from one place to another, day after day.

With every day that passed, the boy realized that life was full of questions without answers. However, one question troubled him the most. How could he help his father dream about good things again and, make those dreams come true?

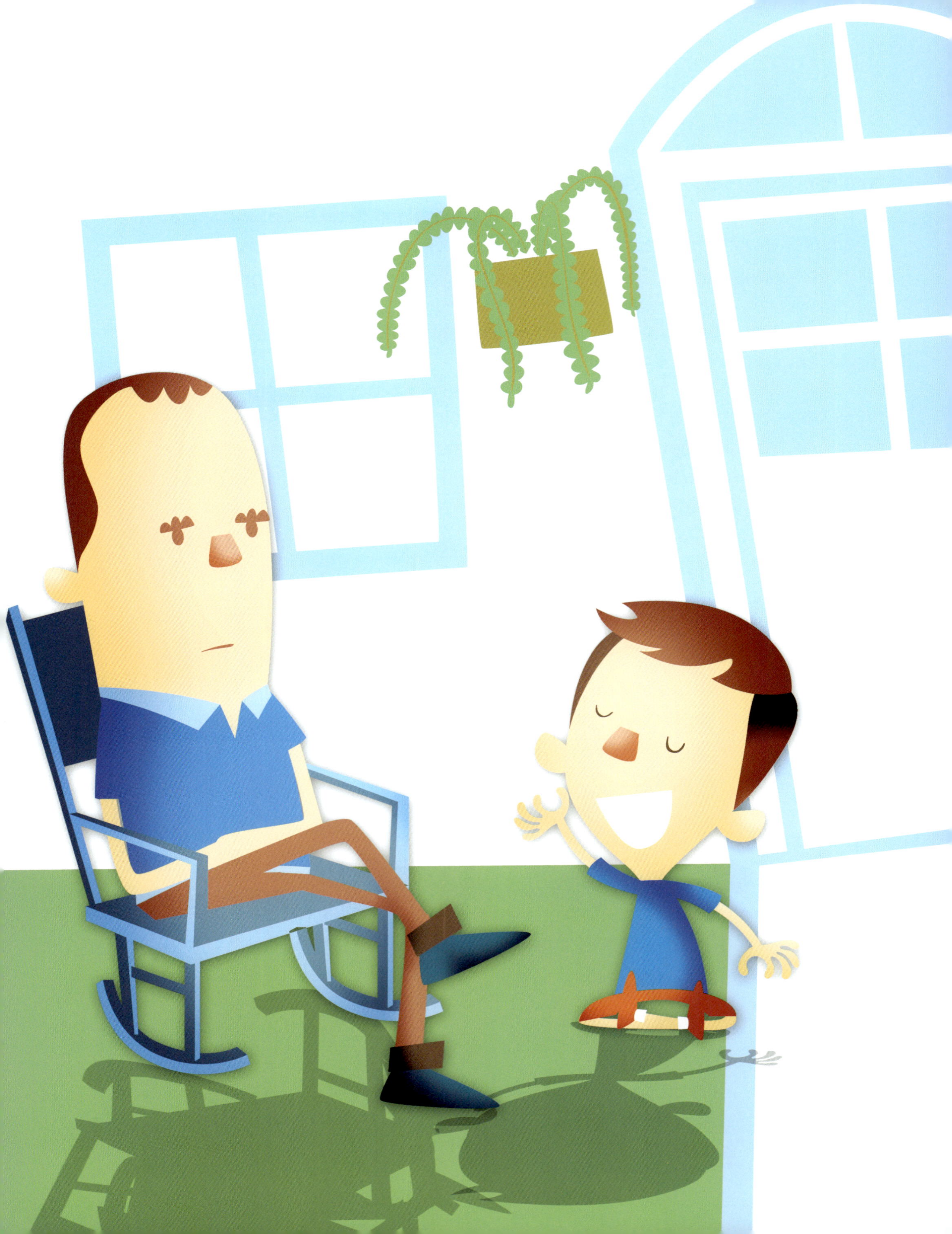

A son's advice

At the end of the day, Ray eagerly waited for his father to arrive home. Keeping a keen lookout from the window, he finally spotted Mr. Unaware coming down the road. His father did not look good. The boy thought it better if he waited for his father to take a shower and eat dinner before they talked.

Before going to bed, Ray walked outside to the porch where his father sat staring at nothing in particular.

Getting up enough courage he asked, "Daddy, why is it you didn't put any coins in your piggy?"

"How come you are asking that question now?" his father replied.

"Because I want you to make your dreams come true."

"I've already told you there's no money left of my salary to save. Now I think it's time you went to bed."

"May I say something else?" insisted the boy.

"Speak up!" answered the father impatiently.

"I've talked to mom and she told me you spend part of your money on foolish things."

"Yes, so what?"

"Well, if you didn't do that, you could be saving and feeding your piggy with coins every single day," Ray advised his father.

At first, Mr. Unaware felt a little awkward but managed to break up the conversation.

"I'll give it some thought, but now you better go to bed. It's late," he told the boy.

So the boy left convinced that the talk with his dad had been unsuccessful. However, he wanted to help his father and to do so, he would wait as long as necessary. After all, as his mother used to say, it was just a matter of patience. Waiting and having patience.

Meanwhile, Mr. Unaware thought over what Ray had told him. In fact, the father realized that sometimes he spent money on things that were not important. He began to give it some serious thought. Perhaps there was something he could do to save money.

Money Boy - Family dreams

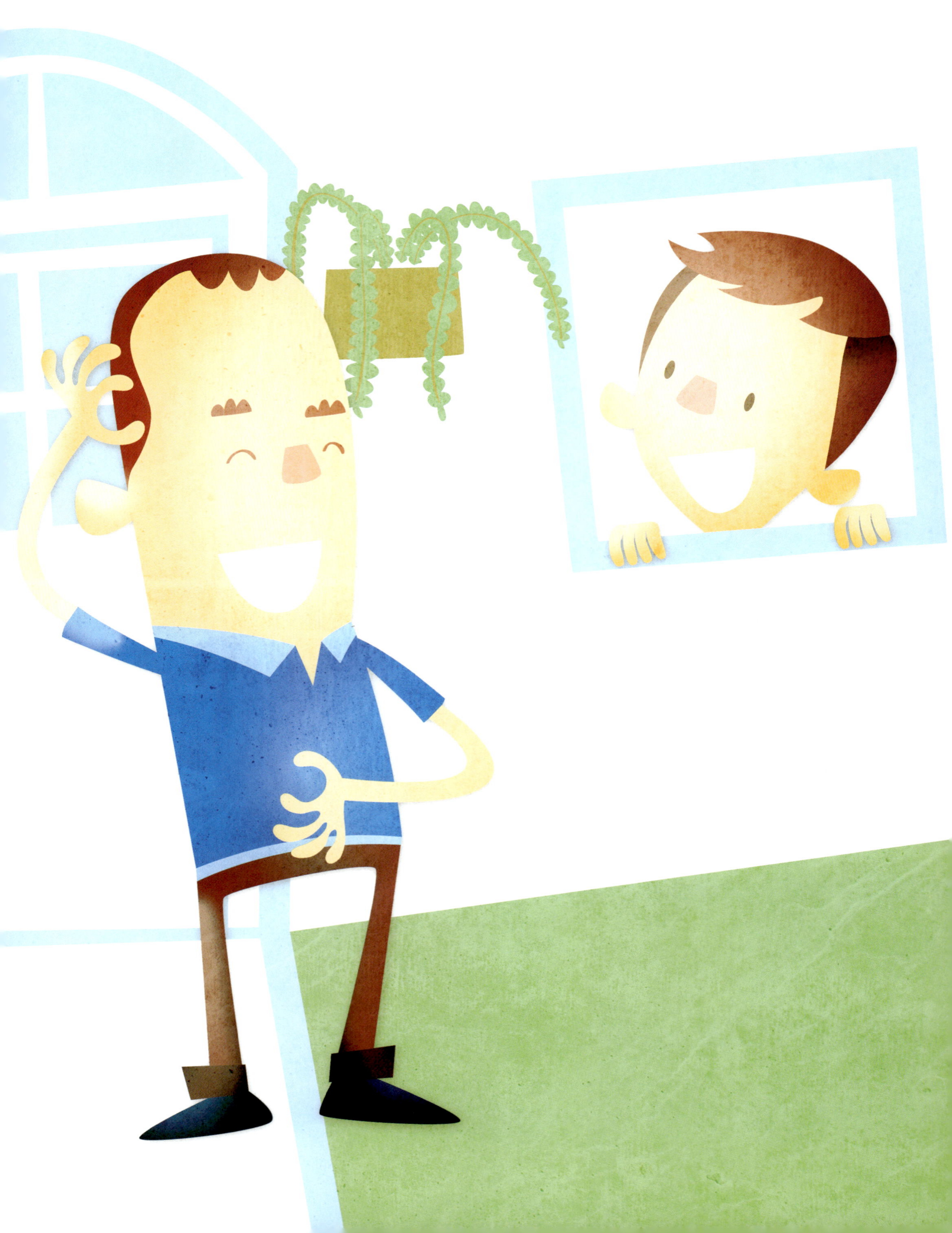

Nothing like a day after another

The day dawned and Ray woke up happy. He jumped out of bed, remembering another phrase his mother used to say repeatedly. "Nothing like a day after another and a good night's sleep between them."

That was exactly how he was feeling. It seemed like good feelings were coming from a place that he didn't quite know where. He had the feeling that good news awaited him.

Ray spent the rest of the day with no major changes in his routine. For a long time he watched a bird carefully building its nest in a tree. Just before dusk, Mr. Unaware arrived home. Ray and his mom were surprised, since his father seldom came home that early. The boy took the opportunity to mention again the subject of the piggy bank.

"Daddy, remember what we talked about yesterday?"

"About what?"

"Your piggy," insisted the boy.

"Oh, yes. So what?" grumbled the father.

"Nothing. Never mind," said the boy, leaving the room with his head hung low.

Mrs. Foresight noticed how upset her son had become and followed him.

"Son, don't be like that. When your father arrives home tired, he doesn't like to chat. What if you two talked after dinner?" she reasoned.

"Would it be any good?" the boy said with a look of doubt on his face.

"Remember what I told you about waiting and being patient?" said Mrs. Foresight.

"All right, mom. I'm not giving up," Ray promised.

Later that evening, the father sat on the porch again and the boy approached him.

"Daddy, can we talk now?" he asked, feeling a little annoyed.

"Yes, son. About what?" answered Mr. Unaware.

"You know, daddy, when I was a kid, I enjoyed buying candy every single day. It was kind of a bad habit I used to have," Ray began.

"Yeah, I know. When you were a kid?"

Mr. Unaware knew what his son was about to ask him, but decided to let the boy finish his story.

"Then mom gave me a piggy bank as a present one day and I started to collect coins inside it. Later on, I got so fond of it that the desire to buy candy every day just vanished.

"And so what?" growled the father.

"Daddy, the piggy I gave you, sitting on your bedside table, is still empty. If you had changed your attitude toward it, you'd have lots of coins by now." the boy summed up.

"I'm used to the way I am and the way I spend my money. It's hard to stop something one has been doing every day for a very long time," the father tried to justify.

"I know, dad. It was hard for me to leave the candy behind, but I made it. You can make it, too. Try to think of something that, if you didn't already own it, it wouldn't make a big difference. Then you'll stop spending on this thing and be able to save your coins to make your dreams come true," Ray insisted.

"I can give it a try, but I'm not sure it's going to work," said the father.

"You can begin trying the way I did with the candy and buy something every other day," suggested the boy.

"Okay, son. I can see that if I don't do what you're telling me to do, you're not going to leave me alone, right?" said the father, with a slight smile.

"Sure, daddy. I'm doing this for your own good," said the boy, trying to imitate the way his mother did when she said things like that.

"You tell me! If you keep talking about it, I'm going to call you Money Boy. How's that?" said the proud father.

Mr. Unaware couldn't help but laugh, observing his son acting like an adviser. Ray, on the other hand, liked the idea of being called Money Boy and enjoyed hearing his father laugh. He could not ever remember hearing his father laughing that much. His little heart felt full of joy and hope. Something told him that nothing would be the same as before.

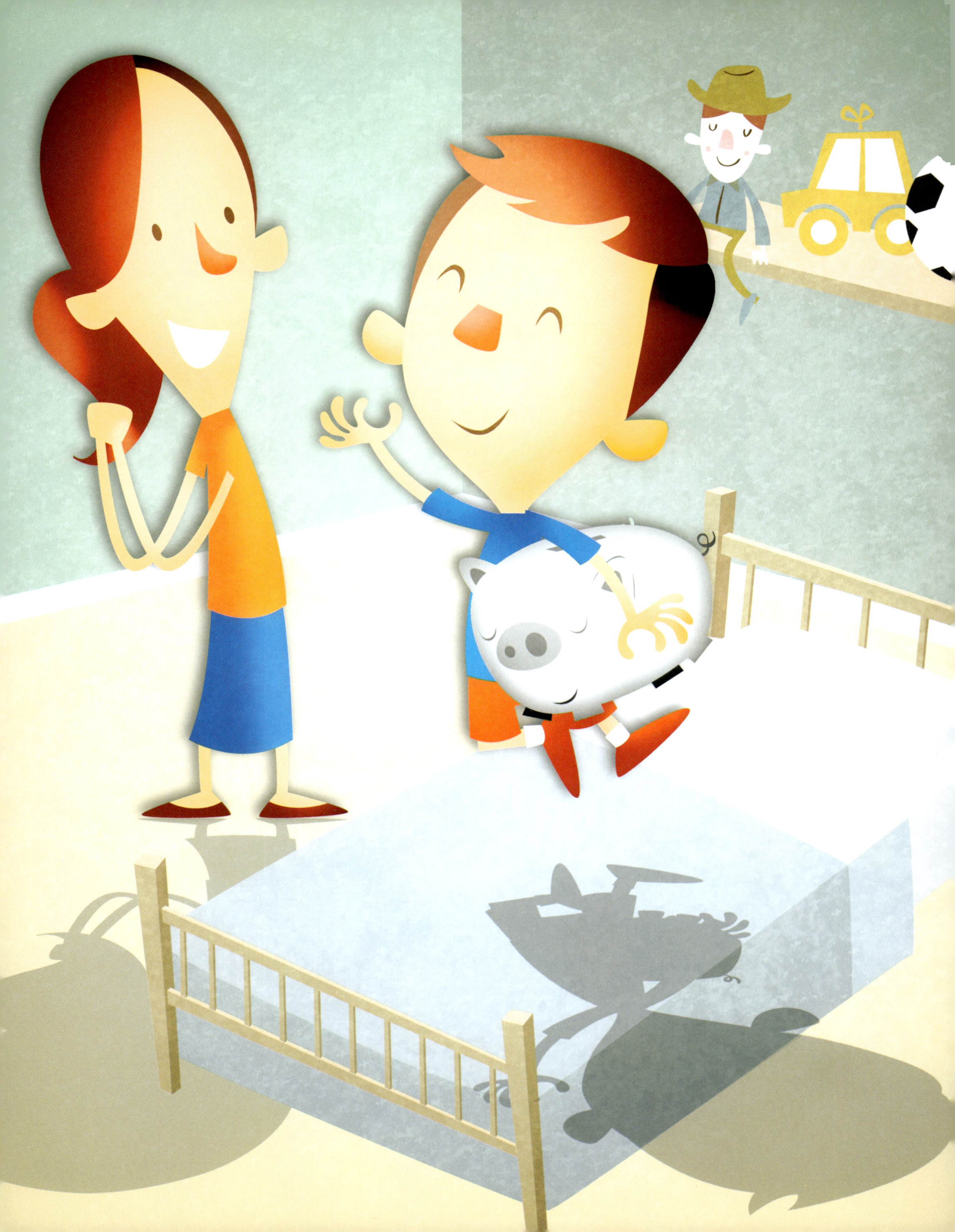

The long-awaited jingling

A few weeks later, the boy woke up with his mother gently running her fingers through his hair.

"What, mom? How come you seem so happy?" he asked while stretching to sit up.

"I came to show you something," she explained.

The boy stood up and rubbing his eyes, he saw his mother holding his father's piggy bank in her hands.

She raised her arms and gently tossed the piggy into the air. Ray heard the coins jingling inside and jumped up and down with excitement.

"We did it, mom! Daddy is really trying to save!

"Yes, son. I noticed him sliding coins into it when he comes home from work."

"Then he's really changed?" said Ray.

"Well, at least he's trying hard," acknowledged the mother.

"I'm really happy! I've helped my daddy. Now he will be able to think about the dreams he wants to come true."

"Remember what I've told you. Everything in its own time!" Mrs. Foresight reminded him.

"That's true, mom. You're always right."

At the end of the day, Mr. Unaware came home to a welcoming and happy son.

"Daddy, your piggy is getting fat. You'll be able to make your dream come true in no time," announced the boy.

"Oh that's true, but let's not rush into things, Money Boy. I have put some coins into it indeed, but I'm not sure for how long I'm going to continue," uttered the father.

"And what are you going to do when it's time to open your piggy? Have you given it any thought yet?" Ray wanted to know.

"Frankly, I don't have a clue. It's been a long while since there was any extra money left that I don't even dream about things any longer," the father said with regret.

"No problem," said Ray. "When your piggy gets full, surely you will have a new dream. I have so many dreams that I am going to need a family of piggies to fulfill all of them."

At that moment, Mrs. Foresight, who was carefully listening, decided to join the conversation.

"Son, today your father has enrolled you in a fine school nearby," she revealed.

"Soon the classes will start and, for your dreams to survive, it will depend on your performance to learn more and more each day."

Watching his son carefully paying attention to what his mother was saying, Mr. Unaware wanted to say something else.

"I have this dream of seeing you studying, learning, and building a better future, brighter than what your mother and I have. It's just that no coins in the world can buy this dream. Everything is up to you, your effort, and your dedication."

As Ray listened to his father, a new world of possibilities emerged in his head. His father, in his simplicity, had given him a powerful lesson. Some dreams can be bought, while others are not for sale.

That night the boy heard a different jingling inside his heart, similar to the noise the coins made inside the piggy bank. Only this sound was stronger, louder, and he would never forget it—the jingling of joy, the belief that every single dream can come true.

Author
Reinaldo Domingos

www.reinaldodomingos.com.br

Reinaldo Domingos is a master degree, professor, educator, and financial therapist. Author of the books: Financial Therapy; Allowance is not just about money; Get rid of debts; I deserve to have money; Money Boy—family dreams; Money Boy—goes to school; Money Boy—friends helping friends; Money Boy—in a sustainable world; Money Boy—little citizen; Money Boy—time for changes; The Boy and the Money; The Boy, the Money, and the Three Piggy Banks; The Boy, the Money, and the Anthopper; Being wealthy is not a secret; and the series Wealth is not a secret.

In 2009 he created Brazil's first textbook series of financial education aimed at grammar school, already in use by several schools in the country, both private and public. In 2012 he was a pioneer in creating the first financial education program for young apprentices. In 2013 that program also included young adults. In 2014 he created the first financial education course for entrepreneurs, followed by financial education as a university extension course.

Domingos graduated in Accounting and System Analysis. He is the founder of Confirp Accounting and Consulting and was the governor of Rotary International District 4610 (2009-2010). Currently, he is the CEO of DSOP Financial Education and DSOP Publishing. He is the mentor, founder and president of Abef (Brazilian Association of Financial Educators). He is also the creator of Brazil's first postgraduate course in Financial Education and Coaching and mentor of the **DSOP Methodology**.

Notes

Notes

Notes

dsop